How to Become a Successful Social Media Marketing Manager

Practical Guide

G. Dellis

Copyright © 2024

Guide to Social Media Marketing Manager

1. Introduction

The introduction to Social Media Marketing is a fundamental concept in the modern digital marketing world. With the advent of social media, companies have the opportunity to reach a vast audience more directly and effectively compared to traditional communication channels.

Social Media Marketing revolves around using social media platforms as tools for communication and promotion for businesses. These channels offer the ability to engage with the audience, build trust relationships, and foster customer loyalty. Additionally, social media enables companies to increase online visibility and reach specific audiences based on interests, age, geographic location, and other demographic factors.

The success of Social Media Marketing depends on businesses' ability to understand and effectively use the various available tools and platforms. Major social media platforms used by businesses include Facebook, Instagram, Twitter, LinkedIn, YouTube, and Pinterest. Each platform has different features and audiences, making it crucial to tailor marketing strategies to maximize results.

Companies have various options to promote their products and services on social media, including creating original content such as posts, videos, and images, managing advertising campaigns, and collaborating with influencers and celebrities. It's also essential to continuously monitor performance metrics and audience engagement to evaluate strategy effectiveness and make necessary adjustments.

Another essential component of Social Media Marketing is managing online reputation. Companies must monitor what is being said about them on social media and respond promptly to customer comments and reviews. Effective customer service on social media can significantly impact how customers perceive the company and influence their purchasing decisions.

Moreover, Social Media Marketing offers companies the opportunity for bidirectional communication with customers, who can provide feedback and suggestions directly through social media. This feedback can be invaluable for improving products and services and building trust with the audience.

Finally, Social Media Marketing also provides the ability to monitor competitors and identify real-time market trends. By analyzing competitor strategies and observing audience reactions to marketing campaigns, companies can adapt their strategies to remain competitive and relevant in the market.

Social Media Marketing is a crucial element for companies aiming to succeed in today's digital world. By strategically and effectively using social media, businesses can increase online visibility, engage with the audience more directly and effectively, enhance online reputation, and stay competitive in the market. With the right strategy and tools, Social Media Marketing can bring significant benefits to businesses of all sectors and sizes.

2. Benefits of Social Media Marketing for Businesses

Social Media Marketing has become an essential part of many companies' marketing strategies, offering a wide range of benefits that can help promote the brand, increase online visibility, generate qualified leads, and improve sales. In this guide, we will explore the key advantages of Social Media Marketing for businesses and how they can best leverage this powerful digital platform to achieve their business goals.

Firstly, Social Media Marketing allows businesses to reach a broader and more diverse audience compared to traditional marketing channels. With billions of active users on platforms like Facebook, Instagram, Twitter, and LinkedIn, businesses can increase their visibility and reach potential customers worldwide. Moreover, advanced targeting offered by social media allows businesses to reach their exact target audience based on interests, demographics, online behaviors, and more, thereby increasing the likelihood of generating qualified leads and conversions.

Another significant advantage of Social Media Marketing is the ability to interact directly with the audience through comments, private messages, and posts. This real-time interaction enables businesses to build more authentic relationships with their customers, listen to their opinions and feedback, and promptly respond to their questions and concerns. This more personal and human approach can help improve customer trust and loyalty, as well as generate greater engagement and participation from the audience.

Social Media Marketing is also a powerful tool for building and strengthening the company's brand. Businesses can use social media to tell their story, share corporate values, promote products and services, and establish a recognizable and distinctive online presence. Furthermore, social media offers a unique opportunity to showcase the human side of the company by sharing behind-the-scenes content, customer success stories, testimonials, and more. This type of authentic and engaging content can help businesses differentiate themselves from competitors and create an emotional connection with their audience.

Moreover, Social Media Marketing is an effective tool for driving traffic to the company's website and increasing visibility in search engines. Regularly sharing high-quality content on social platforms, using relevant keywords, and optimizing business profiles for search engines can help improve search engine rankings and increase organic traffic to the website. Additionally, social media allows businesses to promote sponsored posts and ads to enhance online visibility and reach a wider, targeted audience.

Social Media Marketing can also be an excellent tool for lead generation and customer conversion. Through lead generation strategies such as contests, surveys, special offers, and calls to action, businesses can encourage the audience to provide their contact information and engage with the brand. Furthermore, using remarketing tools and targeted advertising, businesses can reach potential customers who have already shown interest in their products or services, thereby increasing the chances of conversion.

Finally, Social Media Marketing provides businesses with the ability to monitor and measure the results of their campaigns quickly and accurately. By using analytics tools provided by social media platforms, businesses can monitor the performance of their activities, gain insights into what works and what doesn't, and make real-time adjustments. This ability to measure and optimize their social media strategies can help improve campaign effectiveness and maximize return on investment.

In conclusion, Social Media Marketing offers a wide range of benefits for businesses, from small enterprises to large multinational corporations. By wisely using social platforms and adopting effective strategies, businesses can increase their online visibility, generate qualified leads, enhance brand reputation, and boost sales. However, it's important to remember that success in Social Media Marketing depends on a well-defined strategy, consistency in delivering valuable content, and the ability to listen to and engage with the audience authentically and respectfully. With the right approach, Social Media Marketing can become a powerful ally for businesses looking to grow and succeed in today's digital world.

3. Main Tools and Platforms of Social Media Marketing Analysis of Key Social Platforms (Facebook, Instagram, X (formerly Twitter), LinkedIn, Pinterest, YouTube)

Social media and marketing go hand in hand and are increasingly vital for businesses across every sector. In an increasingly digital world, it's crucial to understand and utilize the main tools and platforms of social media marketing to effectively and precisely reach your target audience.

Among the most used and popular social platforms are Facebook, Instagram, Twitter (formerly X), LinkedIn, Pinterest, and YouTube. Each of these platforms has distinct features and characteristics, enabling the dissemination of messages and content in different ways.

Let's start with Facebook, the most widely used social platform globally. With over 2 billion monthly active users, Facebook allows precise and personalized audience targeting through its user profiling capabilities. Businesses can effectively promote their products and services by creating pages and sponsoring posts. Additionally, Facebook offers statistical analysis tools to monitor the performance of advertising campaigns and their impact.

Instagram, owned by Facebook, is primarily a visual-focused platform. With over 1 billion monthly active users, Instagram is highly valued by businesses in fashion, beauty, food, and lifestyle sectors, showcasing their products through high-quality photos and videos. Instagram is also widely used for influencer marketing, where brands collaborate with influencers to promote products and services.

Twitter (formerly X) has long been considered the social network of "here and now," with its brief 280-character messages enabling users to share thoughts, news, and content in real-time.

X is heavily used for customer service, online reputation management, and promoting events and initiatives. Through X Ads, businesses can sponsor tweets and promote accounts to increase visibility on the platform.

LinkedIn is the social platform dedicated to the world of work and business. With over 700 million users worldwide, LinkedIn is widely used by businesses for recruiting qualified personnel, lead generation, and promoting professional content. LinkedIn also allows companies to create business pages, discussion groups, and publish articles and posts to enhance credibility and brand visibility.

Pinterest is a visual-focused social platform centered around creativity. With over 400 million monthly active users, Pinterest is particularly favored by businesses in interior design, home decor, food, and fashion sectors, showcasing their products through mood boards and visual collages. Pinterest is also widely used for content marketing, involving the creation and sharing of quality content to attract and engage users.

Lastly, YouTube is Google's video platform with over 2 billion monthly active users. YouTube is the second-largest search engine globally after Google, allowing users to share and view videos of various kinds. Businesses can use YouTube to create educational videos, tutorials, reviews, and advertisements to promote their products and services. YouTube also offers opportunities to monetize videos through ads and sponsorships.

In addition to the mentioned social platforms, there are dedicated tools and software for social media marketing that enable more efficient and automated management of online communication and promotion activities. Key social media marketing tools include Hootsuite, Buffer, Sprout Social, HubSpot, and SocialBakers. These tools allow for integrated and centralized planning, scheduling, and monitoring of social media activities, saving time and resources.

In conclusion, understanding and utilizing the main tools and platforms of social media marketing is essential for businesses looking to increase their visibility, engagement, and online sales. Through Facebook, Instagram, Twitter (X), LinkedIn, Pinterest, and YouTube, businesses can effectively reach their target audience by creating quality content and continuously monitoring their results. Additionally, using social media marketing tools allows businesses to optimize their online activities and maximize return on investment, contributing to the success and growth of their business.

4. Social Media Management and Monitoring Tools Visual and Video Content Creation Tools

Managing and monitoring social media has become a fundamental practice for businesses aiming to succeed in the digital world. With the increasing online presence and importance of social media, it's essential to use specialized tools that allow businesses to monitor, manage, and analyze their activities across various social channels.

There are numerous tools available on the market that enable effective social media management, including Hootsuite, Buffer, Sprout Social, and many others. These tools allow users to schedule posts, monitor key metrics such as engagement and interactions, manage multiple social accounts simultaneously, and analyze campaign performance.

For instance, Hootsuite is a popular tool that enables management of multiple social media accounts from a single platform, scheduling posts in advance, monitoring conversations, and analyzing data to optimize social media marketing strategies. On the other hand, Buffer allows scheduling posts across various social media channels, team collaboration, and performance analysis of campaigns.

Sprout Social is another comprehensive tool that allows management, monitoring, and analysis of social media performance. With Sprout Social, users can schedule posts, monitor conversations, analyze data, and collaborate with teams to optimize social media marketing strategies.

These tools offer a range of advanced features that enable businesses to effectively manage their presence on social media and achieve tangible results from their online marketing activities. Through these platforms, businesses can create more effective social media marketing strategies, optimize ongoing campaigns, and continuously monitor performance on social media.

In addition to social media management and monitoring tools, it's crucial to use tools for creating visual and video content. With the rise in consumption of visual and video content online, creating engaging and high-quality content is essential to capture audience attention and differentiate from competitors.

There are numerous tools available for creating visual and video content, including Canva, Adobe Spark, Piktochart, Animoto, and many more. These tools allow users to easily create graphics, images, videos, and other compelling visual content for social media and other online channels.

Canva is a very popular tool that allows users to create eye-catching graphics for social media, such as Instagram, Facebook, and Twitter posts, social media covers, presentations, and more. With Canva, users can choose from a wide range of templates and layouts, add text, images, and custom graphics, and quickly share content on social media.

Adobe Spark is another comprehensive tool that allows users to create high-quality visual and video content for social media. With Adobe Spark, users can create graphics, images, videos, and presentations using customizable templates and advanced editing tools.

Piktochart is ideal for creating infographics and compelling graphics for social media. With Piktochart, users can easily create professional infographics using customizable templates, graphic elements, and advanced editing tools.

Animoto is a useful tool for creating engaging videos for social media. With Animoto, users can create high-quality videos using customizable templates, images, videos, and background music to capture audience attention and effectively convey their message.

By using these tools for creating visual and video content, businesses can easily create compelling content for social media and other online channels, differentiate from competitors, and effectively capture audience attention. With high-quality visual content, businesses can increase engagement, improve online visibility, and achieve tangible results from their digital marketing activities.

In conclusion, social media management and monitoring tools, as well as tools for creating visual and video content, are essential for the success of businesses in the digital world. By using these advanced platforms, businesses can effectively manage their presence on social media, create engaging visual content and high-quality videos, and achieve tangible results from their online marketing activities. With the use of appropriate tools, businesses can optimize their social media marketing strategies, increase engagement and online visibility, and differentiate from competitors in an increasingly competitive digital landscape.

5. Defining Social Media Marketing Objectives

Social Media Marketing is a digital marketing strategy focused on using social media to promote a company, brand, or product. Defining social media marketing objectives is crucial for creating a successful strategy and achieving desired outcomes. Objectives can vary based on business needs and goals but generally include increasing brand awareness, user engagement, lead generation, and sales.

Before defining social media marketing objectives, it's important to have a clear understanding of your company, target market, and competitors. Additionally, identifying your target audience and understanding which social media platforms they use most and what types of content they prefer is essential.

Once a comprehensive overview of the current situation is acquired, you can proceed with defining social media marketing objectives. Here are some common objectives that businesses may have:

1. **Increasing Brand Awareness:** One of the primary goals of Social Media Marketing is to enhance brand visibility and introduce potential customers to the products and services offered. To achieve this objective, it's important to create quality content that captures user attention and effectively promotes the brand.

2. **Improving User Engagement:** User engagement on social media is a key indicator of brand health and its ability to engage the audience. Social media marketing objectives may include increasing likes, comments, shares, and interactions with content published by the company.

3. **Generating Qualified Leads:** One of the most important goals of Social Media Marketing is generating qualified leads that can be converted into actual customers. To achieve this objective, businesses can create content that stimulates user interest and encourages them to provide their contact information for further information about the products or services.

4. **Increasing Sales:** Lastly, one of the most critical objectives of Social Media Marketing is to boost sales and generate a positive return on investment for the company. To achieve this objective, promoting special offers, discounts, and exclusive promotions through social media can encourage users to make purchases.

Once social media marketing objectives are defined, it's important to plan a coherent strategy and continually measure the results obtained to assess the effectiveness of the actions taken. Analytical and monitoring tools can be used to measure user engagement, traffic generated from social media, and conversions made through social platforms.

Defining social media marketing objectives is crucial for creating a successful strategy and achieving tangible results. Identifying clear and measurable objectives is essential for guiding social media marketing activities and maximizing return on investment for the company.

6. Defining Content and Engagement Strategies

Content and engagement strategies are crucial in Social Media Marketing. These strategies are essential for improving brand visibility on social media, building relationships with the target audience, increasing engagement, and generating conversions.

Defining content strategies involves ideating and creating valuable and relevant content for the target audience. This content should be useful, interesting, and engaging to attract and maintain user attention over time. Diversifying content types is crucial to keep audience interest alive, including images, videos, text, infographics, webinars, and podcasts.

To define an effective content strategy, it's necessary to:

1. **Know Your Target Audience:** Understanding the behaviors, needs, preferences, and language of your target audience is crucial for creating content that resonates with them and generates engagement.

2. **Set Objectives:** It's important to establish clear and measurable objectives for your content strategy, such as increasing the number of followers, driving website traffic, generating qualified leads, improving brand positioning, and increasing sales.

3. **Identify the Right Channels:** Choosing the most suitable social media channels for your target audience and communication needs is essential. Each social media platform has its own characteristics and peculiarities, so it's important to adapt content and engagement strategies based on the platform used.

Engagement strategies, on the other hand, are crucial for creating a two-way relationship with the audience, actively engaging them, and encouraging participation. Engagement is measured through metrics such as likes, comments, shares, and interactions with content.

To define an effective engagement strategy, it's necessary to:

1. **Create Conversations:** It's important to create authentic conversations with the audience, respond to comments, and actively engage with users in a timely manner.

2. **Engage the Audience:** You can engage the audience with interactive content, polls, contests, questions, influencer marketing, and live streaming.

3. **Monitor and Analyze Results:** It's important to constantly monitor engagement

metrics to assess the effectiveness of your strategies and make any necessary adjustments.

Finally, it's important to always keep in mind that content and engagement strategies should be flexible and adaptable to the needs and reactions of the audience. Testing new ideas, experimenting with new strategies, and continuously monitoring results are crucial for improving the performance of your Social Media Marketing efforts.

7. Planning Social Media Advertising Campaigns

Planning social media advertising campaigns is an essential process for anyone looking to promote their brand, product, or service online. Due to its ability to reach a vast audience of potential customers, social media marketing has become an indispensable tool for businesses across all sectors. However, to achieve effective and lasting results, it's crucial to carefully plan every detail of your social media advertising strategy.

The first step in planning a social media advertising campaign is to define the objectives you want to achieve. These objectives may vary depending on the type of business and specific company needs but typically include increasing brand awareness, generating qualified leads, boosting sales, or engaging with the audience. Once the objectives are set, it's important to identify your target audience, the specific market niche you want to reach. This step is crucial for creating effective and targeted advertising messages that can capture the attention of the right audience.

After defining the objectives and target audience, it's time to choose the social media platforms where you want to promote your advertising campaign. Common choices include Facebook, Instagram, Twitter, LinkedIn, YouTube, and Pinterest, but it's important to carefully assess which platform is most suitable for your business and target audience. For example, if you sell fashion or design products, Instagram might be the best choice due to its visual nature and young, active audience. On the other hand, if it's a B2B company, LinkedIn might be more suitable for reaching industry professionals.

Once the social media platforms are chosen for promoting the advertising campaign, it's crucial to create engaging and high-quality content that can attract the attention of your target audience. This content may include images, videos, written posts, or interactive advertisements, depending on the specific features of the chosen platform. It's also essential to maintain visual and stylistic consistency across all published content to create a recognizable and memorable brand identity.

After creating the content, the next step is to define the budget allocated to the social media advertising campaign. This step is crucial for optimizing the campaign results and ensuring a satisfactory return on investment. It's important to carefully consider how much you're willing to spend on social media advertising and carefully plan the budget allocation across different platforms and types of ads.

Once the budget is defined, it's time to plan the timing of the social media advertising campaign. Choosing the right time to launch your campaign is essential to maximize visibility and impact on your target audience. You can also plan different time phases for content distribution to maintain audience attention in the long term and ensure greater effectiveness of your advertising strategy.

In addition to timing planning, it's also important to constantly monitor the results of your social media advertising campaign to evaluate the effectiveness of your strategies and make any necessary adjustments or improvements. You can use social media analytics tools to monitor campaign success metrics such as impressions, conversion rates, cost per result, and audience engagement. This information is crucial for optimizing your advertising strategies and ensuring the success of your social media campaigns.

Finally, it's important to consider collaborating with influencers or strategic partners to increase the visibility and effectiveness of your social media advertising campaign. Influencers are prominent figures on social media who have high credibility and authority within their niche market and can help promote your brand or product authentically and persuasively. It's important to carefully choose influencers to collaborate with to ensure alignment of values and goals with your brand and target audience.

Planning social media advertising campaigns is a complex but essential process to achieve effective and lasting results in social media marketing. Defining clear objectives, identifying your target audience, choosing the right platforms and content, planning budget and timing, monitoring results, and evaluating collaboration opportunities with influencers are all critical steps to ensure the success of your social media advertising strategy. With careful and thoughtful planning, you can achieve outstanding results and increase the visibility and success of your brand online.

8. Creating and Managing Company Profiles on Social Media

Social media marketing has become an essential element for any company looking to increase its online visibility and reach a broader audience. Creating and managing company profiles on social media are crucial for interacting with customers, promoting products and services, increasing website traffic, and generating high-quality leads for the business.

The first fundamental phase in creating company profiles on social media is identifying the most suitable social networks for your industry and target audience. Each platform has its own characteristics and target audience, so it's important to select those that best suit the company's needs and goals. Major social networks used for social media marketing include Facebook, Instagram, Twitter, LinkedIn, Pinterest, YouTube, and TikTok.

Once the most suitable social networks are identified, it's necessary to create an optimized company profile to maximize visibility and user engagement. Each platform has its own guidelines for creating company profiles, including choosing a recognizable username and profile picture, describing the company and its products/services, and including contact information and links to the website.

Creating original and high-quality content is one of the most important aspects of managing company profiles on social media. Posts should be interesting, useful, and relevant to the target audience to stimulate engagement and generate interest in the company. It's crucial to maintain a consistent and coherent content marketing strategy, which includes publishing organic posts, creating videos, infographics, polls, and interactive surveys, as well as promoting sponsored content through paid ads.

In addition to content production, it's important to actively interact with users and respond promptly to comments, questions, and feedback. Engagement with the audience is essential for building trusted relationships and maintaining a two-way dialogue with customers. Furthermore, it's advisable to constantly monitor post performance and analyze engagement data, reach, click-through rates, and conversion rates to evaluate the effectiveness of the social media marketing strategy and make any necessary improvements.

Promoting company profiles on social media can be done through various online marketing strategies, such as sponsored posts and paid advertising, collaborating with influencers and brand ambassadors, participating in online groups and communities, as well as creating contests, giveaways, and virtual events. It's important to attract attention from the audience and encourage content sharing and dissemination to increase company visibility and generate new high-quality leads.

Finally, managing company profiles on social media requires constant performance monitoring and continuous optimization of the online marketing strategy. It's important to analyze data and measure results to assess the effectiveness of actions taken and identify areas for improvement. Additionally, it's advisable to test new strategies and approaches to keep your online presence fresh and aligned with market trends.

Creating and managing company profiles on social media are crucial for increasing online visibility and engagement with the audience. Investing in creating quality content, interacting with the audience, and promoting company profiles allows you to achieve significant results and generate new business opportunities. With an effective and well-structured social media marketing strategy, you can build a strong brand, retain existing customers, and attract new prospects interested in the company's products and services.

9. Monitoring Activities and Performance Indicators

Monitoring activities and performance indicators in Social Media Marketing is a fundamental process to evaluate the effectiveness of adopted strategies and measure the success of online campaigns. Thanks to analytics and monitoring tools, it's possible to gather valuable data to assess the performance of social media activities, identify strengths and weaknesses in campaigns, and make corrections to improve results.

Monitoring activities on social media involves gathering information on user interactions with content, such as the number of views, likes, comments, shares, and post interactions. These data points allow for evaluating audience engagement and understanding which types of content perform best in achieving predefined objectives.

Various analytics tools can be used to monitor social media activities, such as Google Analytics, Facebook Insights, Twitter Analytics, and LinkedIn Analytics. These tools provide detailed insights into page and social profile performance, enabling monitoring of metrics like follower count, growth rate, engagement rate, reach, and conversions generated from campaigns.

In addition to activity monitoring, it's crucial to track performance indicators (KPIs) to evaluate the effectiveness of Social Media Marketing strategies. Performance indicators are metrics that measure campaign success and assess return on investment. Some examples of KPIs in Social Media Marketing include conversion rate, cost per lead acquired, engagement rate, reach, and brand awareness.

To monitor performance indicators effectively, clear and measurable objectives must be defined. It's essential to establish which metrics are most meaningful for evaluating campaign success and utilize specific analytics tools to track and analyze data. Constant analysis of achieved results, comparison with predefined objectives, and making any necessary corrections or optimizations to strategies are important steps to improve performance.

One of the crucial aspects of monitoring activities and performance indicators in Social Media Marketing is analyzing collected data and interpreting it. It's important not only to monitor numbers but also to critically analyze data to understand trends, identify factors influencing performance, and pinpoint improvement opportunities.

Monitoring activities and performance indicators in Social Media Marketing is an essential process to evaluate the effectiveness of adopted strategies, measure the success of online campaigns, and make corrections to optimize results. Utilizing analytics and monitoring tools allows for gathering detailed information on social media performance and making informed decisions to improve ROI and achieve business objectives.

10. Responding to User Interactions and Crisis Management

Social media marketing is a critical part of any successful digital marketing strategy, but managing user interactions and crises on social media can be challenging. It's important to have a detailed plan on how to manage these situations quickly and effectively to protect the brand's reputation and maintain positive communication with the audience.

In managing user interactions on social media, it's crucial to be prepared to respond promptly to comments, questions, and follower feedback. Providing timely and quality customer service on social media can build stronger bonds with the audience and increase trust in your brand. Promptly addressing customer inquiries, even if they are criticisms or negative reviews, demonstrates that you care about customer feedback and are willing to resolve any issues.

It's also important to be authentic and transparent in social media interactions. Responding honestly and openly to customer inquiries, without hiding information or attempting to manipulate the conversation, helps build a reputation for transparency and honesty for your brand. Additionally, showing a human and personal side in how you respond to user interactions can help create a more authentic and genuine relationship with the audience.

Another critical aspect of managing user interactions on social media is being mindful of the tone and style of online communication. Adapting your response tone based on the type of interaction and the involved audience can ensure the message is received correctly. For example, when responding to a negative review, it's important to remain calm and respond professionally, without descending to the level of criticism or accusations.

Furthermore, continuously monitoring user interactions on social media is essential to quickly identify any issues or criticisms so that prompt action can be taken. Using social media conversation monitoring tools can help quickly spot negative comments or potential crises in their early stages, allowing you to address them before they escalate into a bigger problem.

When it comes to managing crises on social media, it's crucial to have a well-defined emergency plan in place in advance. This plan should include detailed procedures on how to handle specific crisis situations, such as responding to negative comments, managing issue escalation, and communicating with the audience during a crisis. Having a well-structured emergency plan can help reduce the risk of brand reputation damage during a crisis and enable effective and professional crisis management.

During a social media crisis, it's important to be transparent with the audience and communicate clearly and promptly about what is happening and what steps are being taken to resolve the situation. Keeping followers informed and engaged during a crisis can help mitigate damage to the brand's reputation and demonstrate active management of the situation.

Additionally, it's important to take customer concerns and criticisms seriously during a crisis and work to find appropriate solutions and responses. Listening carefully to customers and demonstrating empathy can help rebuild trust and restore the brand's reputation after a crisis.

Finally, learning from past crises and using these experiences to improve and strengthen crisis management strategies is crucial. Analyzing lessons learned from previous crisis situations and making necessary adjustments to the emergency plan can help ensure the brand is well-prepared to handle any challenging situations on social media in the future.

Managing user interactions and crises on social media is a crucial aspect of social media marketing that requires planning, responsiveness, and transparency. Responding promptly to user interactions, being authentic and transparent in online communication, adapting tone and style to different situations, continuously monitoring conversations, and having an emergency plan are all key strategies for successfully managing user interactions and crises on social media. Treating criticisms and crises as opportunities to improve and strengthen the brand's reputation can help build a stronger relationship with the audience and ensure long-term success of social media marketing.

11. Creating Effective Content for Social Media

In recent years, Social Media Marketing has become a fundamental tool for businesses looking to promote their products and services, reach a wide audience, and interact directly and instantly with customers. One key to success on these platforms is creating effective content that captures users' attention and generates interest and engagement.

To create effective content for social media, it's important to have a well-defined strategy and carefully plan each post. First and foremost, understanding your target audience and knowing their interests, online habits, and preferred platforms is crucial. Only then can you create content that resonates with them and drives positive interactions.

Another aspect to consider is brand consistency. Maintaining a consistent tone of voice and aesthetic across different social media platforms helps in being easily recognizable and memorable to your followers. Additionally, creating original and creative content that stands out from the competition and captures users' attention is important.

A good practice is to vary the types of content published, including photos, videos, polls, stories, and textual posts. This provides greater variety to users and encourages interaction. It's also advisable to use relevant hashtags and create shareable content that evokes emotions among followers.

Publishing frequency is another crucial aspect not to be underestimated. It's important to maintain a consistent presence on social media without overwhelming your audience with too many posts. Finding the right balance is essential to avoid being invasive and boring your followers.

Finally, it's important to constantly monitor

the results and analyze the performance of your content. There are various tools available to measure the effectiveness of your social media marketing activities, such as Google Analytics and Insights from various social media platforms. Analyzing data allows you to understand what works and what doesn't, and make necessary adjustments to improve your results.

Creating effective content for social media is a critical step to succeed on these platforms. By following the right guidelines and carefully planning your activities, you can generate engagement, increase brand awareness, and achieve concrete results for your business.

12. Most Effective Content Types on Each Social Media Platform

Social media marketing has become a crucial tool for businesses aiming to reach and engage their target audience. Each social media platform has different characteristics and functionalities, so it's important to tailor content accordingly.

Here's an overview of the most effective content types on each social media platform:

1. **Facebook:**

   - **Visual Content:** Images and videos are crucial on Facebook as they capture users' attention and increase engagement.

   - **Live Streaming:** Live videos allow businesses to interact in real-time with their audience and build a closer relationship.

   - **Contests and Giveaways:** Organizing contests and giving away prizes is an excellent way to engage users and increase visibility.

2. **Instagram:**

   - **High-Quality Images:** Instagram is a visual platform, so images should be curated and of high quality.

   - **Stories:** Stories are very popular on Instagram and allow sharing of content in vertical and temporary formats.

   - **Influencer Collaborations:** Collaborating with influencers can help reach a wider audience and enhance brand credibility.

3. **Twitter:**

   - **Short and Punchy Tweets:** On Twitter, it's important to be concise and direct to capture users' attention quickly.

   - **Hashtags:** Using relevant hashtags can increase tweet visibility and reach a broader audience.

   - **Viral Content:** Sharing viral and current content can help generate engagement and increase shares.

4. **LinkedIn:**

   - **Professional Content:** Share relevant and professional content on LinkedIn that aligns with your business image.

   - **Thought Leadership Articles:** Sharing thought leadership articles can help position the company as an industry expert.

   - **Networking and Collaborations:** LinkedIn is perfect for connecting with industry professionals and creating collaborations.

5. **YouTube:**

   - **Tutorial Videos:** Creating tutorial and guide videos can demonstrate expertise and credibility.

   - **Behind-the-Scenes Videos:** Sharing behind-the-scenes videos allows users to get to know the company and its processes better.

   - **Collaborations with Content Creators:** Collaborating with YouTubers and influencers can increase video visibility and attract a larger audience.

6. **TikTok:**

   - **Fun and Creative Content:** TikTok is entertainment-focused, so creating fun and creative content is essential to engage users.

   - **Challenges:** Creating challenges and encouraging users to participate can increase engagement and brand visibility.

   - **Music and Sounds:** Using popular music and sounds in videos can increase content virality and attract new followers.

To succeed in social media marketing, it's crucial to create content tailored to the chosen platform and target audience. Leveraging the features and functionalities of different platforms can help businesses achieve their marketing goals and build a closer relationship with their followers.

13. Best Practices for Creating Visual and Video Content

Visual and video content is becoming increasingly important in the world of social media marketing. With the rise of online competition, it is crucial to create content that captures the audience's attention and engages them significantly. In this article, we will explore best practices for creating effective visual and video content for social media marketing.

1. Know your target audience: Before creating any type of visual or video content, it is essential to understand your target audience. What are their interests, needs, and consumption preferences? Use demographic and behavioral information to create content that resonates with your audience and generates meaningful engagement.

2. Create original and unique content: To stand out from the competition, it's important

to create original and unique visual and video content. Avoid copying your competitors and strive to create something new and innovative that captures the audience's attention. Use your creativity to craft memorable and distinctive content.

3. Use compelling storytelling: Storytelling is a powerful way to engage the audience and create an emotional connection with your brand. Use compelling narratives in your video content to authentically convey the brand's values and mission. Tell stories that resonate with the audience and inspire them to take action.

4. Optimize your content for each platform: Each social media platform has different requirements for visual and video content. Make sure to optimize your content for each platform by adjusting dimensions, duration, and format according to specific needs. This will ensure that your content is displayed correctly and generates optimal engagement.

5. Focus on content quality: Content quality is fundamental to the success of social media marketing. Ensure that you create high-quality visual and video content with good resolution and clear audio. Invest in high-quality production tools and resources to ensure that your content stands out on social media platforms.

6. Use music and audio effectively: Music and audio can significantly enhance the video experience and engage the audience more deeply. Carefully choose the soundtrack for your videos and ensure that it aligns with the tone and purpose of the content. Use audio effects and sound design to create an engaging experience for the audience.

7. Include a clear call to action: Every visual or video content should include a clear call to action to guide the audience towards a specific action. Whether it's subscribing, sharing, or making a purchase, make sure to provide your audience with a clear indication of what they should do after viewing the content. This will

increase engagement and conversions.

8. Collaborate with influencers and content creators: Collaborating with influencers and content creators is a great way to expand the reach of your visual and video content. Seek partnerships with prominent figures in your industry or content creators with a relevant audience. This will help you reach new audience segments and increase brand awareness.

9. Monitor and analyze the performance of your content: It is essential to monitor and analyze the performance of your visual and video content to understand what works and what doesn't. Use analytics tools to track metrics such as views, engagement, shares, and conversions. Use this information to optimize your content and improve performance in the future.

Creating effective visual and video content for social media marketing requires a strategic and targeted approach. Use these best practices to create content that captures the audience's attention, generates engagement, and contributes to the success of your brand online. Harness the power of visual and video content to create a lasting impact on the audience and differentiate yourself from the competition.

14. Tools for Creating and Scheduling Content

In the digital era, Social Media Marketing plays a crucial role for businesses looking to promote their products and services, interact with customers, and increase their online visibility. To achieve effective results and reach your target audience, it is necessary to use advanced tools for creating and scheduling content.

One of the first steps to a successful Social Media Marketing strategy is choosing the right tool for content creation. There are numerous platforms that allow you to create compelling images, high-quality videos, infographics, and more. Among the most popular are Canva, Adobe Spark, Piktochart, and Snappa. These tools offer a wide range of customizable templates, fonts, colors, and graphics to create visually appealing content that effectively communicates the company's message.

When it comes to video creation, it's important to use professional tools such as Adobe Premiere Pro, Final Cut Pro, or Filmora to ensure high quality and significant visual impact. These software programs allow you to edit videos, add special effects, transitions, and subtitles to create compelling and engaging content for social media.

Once your content is created, scheduling is essential. Using a social media management tool like Hootsuite, Buffer, Sprout Social, or Socialbakers allows you to schedule posts in advance, monitor engagement, analyze performance, and efficiently manage all social profiles of the company. These tools save time, optimize online presence, and constantly monitor the performance of Social Media Marketing campaigns.

To ensure consistency and cohesion in your Social Media Marketing strategy, it is essential to use tools for content creation and scheduling that allow you to schedule posts according to the best times for your target audience, monitor campaign performance, and adjust the strategy in real-time based on results. This way, you can maximize the impact of your presence on social media and achieve predefined marketing goals.

In addition to content creation and scheduling tools, there are advanced tools for managing advertising campaigns on social media. Platforms like Facebook Ads Manager, Google Ads, LinkedIn Ads, and Twitter Ads offer functionalities for creating targeted ads, monitoring campaign performance, and optimizing results based on the company's marketing goals. With these tools, you can effectively reach your target audience, increase online visibility, and generate qualified leads for your business.

The use of tools for content creation and scheduling is essential for a successful Social Media Marketing strategy. Thanks to these advanced platforms, you can create high-quality visual content, schedule posts in advance, monitor campaign performance, and optimize results in real-time. With a well-defined strategy and the use of the right tools, businesses can achieve effective results and maximize their impact on social media.

15. Performance Analysis and Reporting

Definition of Key Performance Indicators (KPIs) for Social Media Marketing

Social Media Marketing is a digital marketing strategy that uses social media platforms to promote a company's products or services. To assess the effectiveness of a Social Media Marketing campaign, it is crucial to define Key Performance Indicators (KPIs). KPIs are quantitative measures that allow monitoring and evaluating the progress and success of a Social Media Marketing campaign.

KPIs in Social Media Marketing can vary depending on the company's objectives and the adopted strategy. However, there are common KPIs used to evaluate the performance of a Social Media Marketing campaign, including:

1. Reach: The breadth of the campaign's

coverage on social media. This KPI measures the number of people who have viewed the content posted by the company.

2. Engagement: User interaction with content posted on social media, such as likes, comments, shares, and link clicks. High engagement indicates that the posted content is interesting and engaging for the audience.

3. Follower growth: The increase in the number of followers on the company's social media accounts. This KPI indicates the campaign's effectiveness in generating interest and engagement from the audience.

4. Conversion rate: The percentage of users who perform a desired action, such as purchasing a product or filling out a form, after being exposed to the Social Media Marketing campaign.

5. Click-through rate (CTR): The percentage of users who click on links in content posted on social media. A high CTR indicates that the content is relevant and interesting to the audience.

Once the performance indicators are defined, it is essential to constantly monitor the results of the Social Media Marketing campaign and create periodic reports to evaluate its effectiveness and make any necessary adjustments and improvements. Reporting in Social Media Marketing is an essential tool for monitoring and evaluating campaign performance and making informed decisions about the strategy to adopt.

Social Media Marketing reports should be clear, detailed, and capable of providing useful information on campaign performance. Some elements that should be included in Social Media Marketing reports are:

1. KPI analysis: A summary of the key performance indicators and evaluation of the results achieved compared to the set objectives.

2. Performance trends: Analysis of KPI trends over time to identify any significant trends and variations.

3. Competitive analysis: Comparison of the performance of your campaign with that of key competitors to assess competitiveness and identify improvement opportunities.

4. Content analysis: Evaluation of the performance of different types of content posted on social media to identify those that generate higher engagement and conversions.

5. Demographic analysis: Analysis of the campaign's target audience to better understand user preferences and behaviors and adapt the Social Media Marketing strategy

accordingly.

Furthermore, it is important for Social Media Marketing reports to be customized based on the company's goals and needs. For example, if the campaign's goal is to increase sales, the report should focus on KPIs related to conversion and ROI (Return on Investment). If the goal is to increase brand awareness, the focus should be on KPIs related to reach and engagement.

Performance indicators and reporting are fundamental tools for evaluating the effectiveness of a Social Media Marketing campaign and guiding the company's strategic decisions. Constantly monitoring results, analyzing data, and making any necessary corrections and optimizations are crucial actions to maximize the success of your Social Media Marketing strategy.

16. Monitoring campaign and brand performance on social media

In today's digital world, monitoring the performance of campaigns and brand on social media plays a fundamental role in the success of any social media marketing strategy. With the increasing number of active users on platforms such as Facebook, Instagram, Twitter, and LinkedIn, it is essential for companies to constantly monitor the effectiveness of their campaigns and the sentiment towards their brand in order to adapt their strategies in a timely and effective manner.

Monitoring the performance of campaigns on social media is based on a series of key indicators, including user engagement, the number of clicks on published content, the conversion rate of advertising, and the growth of followers. These data provide companies with a clear overview of the performance of their campaigns and allow them to evaluate the effectiveness of the strategies adopted.

One of the most used tools for monitoring campaign performance on social media is Google Analytics, which allows tracking traffic from social media and analyzing data related to user engagement and conversions. Additionally, social media platforms themselves provide performance analysis tools, such as Facebook Insights and Instagram Insights, which allow monitoring the performance of advertising campaigns and user interaction with published content.

In addition to monitoring campaign performance, it is equally important to monitor the sentiment towards the brand on social media. Through the analysis of conversations and user comments, companies can assess the public opinion towards their brand and identify any critical issues to address. Sentiment monitoring can be done using social listening tools such as Hootsuite and Brandwatch, which allow monitoring brand mentions on social media and analyzing the tone and content of conversations.

Furthermore, sentiment monitoring can also be used to identify trends and topics of interest for the target audience, in order to create content that resonates with the audience and generates greater engagement. For example, if through sentiment analysis, a growing interest in a specific topic is identified among the brand's followers, companies can create related content to stimulate the interest of their target audience.

In addition to monitoring campaign and sentiment performance, it is important to also monitor competitor activity on social media. Analyzing the strategies adopted by competitors and comparing them with their own performance can provide valuable information to improve social media marketing strategies and remain competitive in the market. Additionally, monitoring competitors allows companies to identify potential collaboration or partnership opportunities to expand their audience and reach new potential customers.

Monitoring campaign and brand performance on social media is a fundamental element for the success of companies' social media marketing strategies. Through constant analysis of data and user sentiment, companies can adapt their strategies in a timely and effective manner, generating greater engagement and loyalty from their target audience. With the help of analysis tools and social listening, companies can obtain a clear overview of performance on social platforms and create targeted content that generates tangible results for the business.

17. Creation of periodic reports and analysis of results

The analysis of results and the creation of periodic reports are two fundamental aspects for evaluating the effectiveness of a Social Media Marketing strategy. This process allows monitoring the progress of activities carried out on different social channels, identifying any issues, and making corrections to improve performance.

Starting with the analysis of results, it is important to define clear and measurable objectives to be achieved through social media marketing activities. These objectives may include increasing the number of followers, enhancing interaction and engagement with the audience, generating leads, or selling products or services.

Once the objectives are defined, it is necessary to use analytics tools such as Google Analytics, Facebook Insights, X Analytics,

LinkedIn Analytics, and other specific platforms of the social media used. These tools provide detailed data on page performance, user behavior, and campaign effectiveness.

A crucial step is to analyze basic metrics such as the number of followers, engagement rate, reach, and interactions with published content. These data allow evaluating community growth and audience engagement with shared content.

Furthermore, it is essential to monitor the performance of advertising campaigns, evaluating conversion rates, cost per conversion, return on investment (ROI), and other metrics related to defined business objectives. This helps to understand if advertising campaigns are generating positive results and optimize spending to maximize outcomes.

In addition to quantitative metrics, it is important to analyze qualitative feedback received from followers through comments, messages, and reviews. This feedback provides valuable insights into the appreciation of shared content, and the needs and desires of the target audience.

Once all available data is collected and analyzed, it is important to create periodic reports that summarize the results obtained clearly and concisely. Reports can be weekly, monthly, quarterly, or annual, depending on the company's needs.

Periodic reports should include a summary of performance achieved compared to set objectives, highlighting key metrics and variations from previous periods. Additionally, it is useful to include comparative analyses with competitors to assess the company's position in the market and identify opportunities for improvement.

Reports should be customized based on client or company needs, including recommendations and suggestions to enhance future performance.

Ultimately, the analysis of results and creation of periodic reports should be an integral part of a continuous optimization and improvement process of social media marketing strategies. Only through constant and accurate data analysis can corrective actions be identified to maximize results and achieve set objectives.

18. Strategies

With the increase in consumer use of social media, companies must be present and active on platforms such as Facebook, Instagram, Twitter, LinkedIn, and others. In this article, we will examine 40 effective Social Media Marketing strategies to help businesses achieve positive results on social platforms.

1. Define objectives: Before starting any Social Media Marketing campaign, it is important to clearly define the goals you want to achieve. These goals may include increasing website traffic, boosting sales, generating leads, increasing engagement, and so on.

2. Know your target audience: It is important to have a deep understanding of your target audience, including demographic information, interests, online behaviors, preferences, and purchasing habits. This knowledge will help create targeted content and direct advertising

campaigns more effectively.

3. Choose the right platforms: Not all social media platforms are suitable for all businesses. It is important to identify the platforms that are most suitable for your industry and target audience and focus on them to maximize Social Media Marketing efforts.

4. Create an editorial plan: An editorial plan is essential for planning and organizing content to be shared on social media. The editorial plan should include content types, posting frequency, conversion goals, and budget for content promotion.

5. Create quality content: Quality content is key to Social Media Marketing success. It is important to create relevant, interesting, and useful content for your target audience, using text, images, videos, and other multimedia formats.

6. Use social media advertising: Social media advertising is an effective way to increase content visibility and engagement. Platforms like Facebook Ads, Instagram Ads, Twitter Ads, and LinkedIn Ads offer advanced targeting options to reach your target audience more effectively.

7. Collaborate with influencers: Collaborating with influencers is an effective way to increase visibility and engagement on social media. Influencers have a dedicated and trusting audience that can be engaged through paid partnerships and collaborations.

8. Monitor and analyze results: It is important to constantly monitor the performance of Social Media Marketing campaigns and analyze the results obtained. This will help identify what works and what does not, and optimize marketing strategies to maximize results.

9. Use relevant hashtags: Hashtags are important for increasing content visibility on social media. It is important to use relevant and popular hashtags to reach a wider audience and increase engagement.

10. Responding to comments and interactions: It is important to be active and responsive on social media, responding to comments, questions, and interactions promptly. This shows care and attention towards the audience and helps to build a trusting relationship with followers.

11. Creating contests and giveaways: Contests and giveaways are an effective way to increase engagement and generate interest around the brand. It is important to plan creative and attractive contests, offering interesting prizes to encourage participation.

12. Collaborating with other companies and brands: Collaborating with other companies and brands can lead to mutual benefits,

increasing visibility and engagement on social media. You can organize partnerships, joint events, giveaways, and other collaboration initiatives to reach new audiences.

13. Creating evergreen content: Evergreen content is timeless and always relevant to the target audience. Creating evergreen content allows you to continue generating engagement over time, increasing traffic and visibility on social media.

14. Using Stories: Stories are a popular feature on platforms like Instagram, Facebook, and Snapchat. Using Stories to share temporary and authentic content engages the audience more directly and immediately.

15. Hosting webinars and live events: Webinars and live events are an effective way to interact and engage with the audience in real-time. Hosting online events allows you to reach a broader audience and create an engaging experience for followers.

16. Creating visual content: Visual content, such as images and videos, is more engaging and attractive than simple text. Using high-quality visual content captures the audience's attention and increases engagement on social media.

17. Implementing retargeting: Retargeting is an effective technique to reach people who have already interacted with the brand on social media or the website. Using retargeting to show targeted ads to people who have shown interest in your products or services.

18. Consistent publishing: Consistency is crucial for maintaining engagement and audience loyalty on social media. Publishing consistently, maintaining a regular posting frequency will help keep the brand at the top of followers' minds.

19. Creating an online community: Building an online community around your brand is an effective way to increase engagement and

audience loyalty. Engaging followers, creating discussions, and promoting interactions among community members will create a stronger bond with the brand.

20. Using social media for customer service: Social media can be used as a customer service channel to respond to questions, assistance requests, and complaints promptly. Resolving customer issues on social media will improve the brand's reputation and increase audience trust.

21. Creating educational content: Creating educational and informative content on social media is an effective way to position yourself as an expert in your industry and provide added value to your target audience. Tutorials, guides, and informative resources will be appreciated by followers and help generate interest around the brand.

22. Measuring campaign ROI: It is important to measure the Return on Investment (ROI) of

Social Media Marketing campaigns to evaluate the effectiveness of strategies and optimize investments more targeted. Use analytics and tracking tools to monitor campaign performance and evaluate results.

23. Collaborating with local influencers: Collaborating with local influencers is an effective way to reach a geographically specific audience and increase brand visibility in targeted areas. Local influencers have a dedicated and engaged follower base that can be used to promote local products or services.

24. Using analytics tools: Analytics tools are essential for monitoring the performance of Social Media Marketing campaigns and obtaining useful insights on audience behavior, engagement, and conversions. Use tools like Google Analytics, Facebook Insights, and Instagram Insights to track key metrics and evaluate results.

25. Leveraging reviews and testimonials: Positive reviews and testimonials are important for the brand's online reputation and acquiring new customers. Use reviews and testimonials on social media to show customer satisfaction and promote trust in the brand.

26. Creating user-generated content: User-generated content is authentic and engaging, and can help build a stronger relationship with the audience. Encourage followers to share user-generated content, such as photos, videos, and reviews, to increase engagement and trust in the brand.

27. Creating storytelling campaigns: Storytelling is an effective strategy to emotionally engage the audience and create a deeper connection with the brand. Sharing relevant and engaging stories on social media will capture followers' attention and create an emotional bond with the brand.

28. Collaborating with associations and non-profit organizations: Collaborating with associations and non-profit organizations is an effective way to demonstrate the brand's social and environmental commitment and promote important causes on social media. Participating in charity initiatives and supporting significant causes will improve the brand's image and increase audience engagement.

29. Organizing themed events and contests: Organizing themed events and contests on social media is a fun and engaging way to interact with the audience and increase engagement. Creating events and contests related to holidays, celebrations, or specific themes will generate interest around the brand and actively engage followers.

30. Collaborating with micro-influencers: Collaborating with micro-influencers is an opportunity to reach a smaller but highly engaged audience interested in your industry. Micro-influencers have a smaller but highly

loyal following that can be engaged more directly and authentically.

31. Using geotargeting: Using geotargeting on social media is an effective way to reach a local and geographically specific audience. Using location tags and publishing localized content will increase brand visibility in targeted areas.

32. Creating viral content: Creating viral content on social media is an ambitious but rewarding goal. Creating creative, fun, original, and relevant content that can be widely shared by the audience will increase brand visibility and engagement.

33. Using shopping features: Shopping features on platforms like Instagram and Facebook allow you to tag products and facilitate direct purchases from followers. Using shopping features to promote products and services will increase direct conversions from social media.

34. Collaborating with brand ambassadors: Collaborating with brand ambassadors is an effective way to promote the brand through influential and trusted personalities. Ambassadors can promote the brand, participate in events and marketing initiatives, and create dedicated content for the brand on social media.

35. Using video marketing: Video marketing is one of the most effective strategies to engage the audience and generate interest around the brand. Creating high-quality, interesting, and informative videos will increase engagement and communicate more effectively with followers.

36. Creating interactive content: Interactive content, such as polls, quizzes, questions and answers, is an effective way to actively engage the audience and generate participation. Creating interactive content on social media will capture followers' attention and increase engagement.

37. Using remarketing: Remarketing is an effective technique to reach people who have visited the website but have not completed a desired action, such as a purchase or registration. Use remarketing on social media to show targeted ads to interested people who may be more likely to convert.

38. Optimizing social profiles: Optimizing company social profiles is important to increase visibility and audience trust. Update cover images, profile pictures, contact information, and descriptions to ensure profiles accurately reflect the brand's identity and values.

39. Planning seasonal campaigns: Planning seasonal Social Media Marketing campaigns is an effective way to capitalize on holidays, celebrations, and cultural events. Creating thematic content and promoting special offers during key periods will increase engagement and conversions.

40. Collaborating with podcasts and voice influencers: Collaborating with podcasts and voice influencers is an effective way to reach an audience interested in listening and audio. Participating in partnerships with podcasts and voice content creators will promote the brand through alternative and innovative channels.

Social Media Marketing is one of the most important strategies for companies wishing to reach and engage their online audience. By using the 40 effective Social Media Marketing strategies listed in this article, companies can maximize their success on social media and achieve positive results in terms of visibility, engagement, conversions, and customer loyalty.

19. Analysis of Adopted Strategies and Achieved Results

Through social media, it's possible to reach a vast audience, interact with customers, and create a solid and engaging online presence. In this context, the strategies adopted and the results achieved play a crucial role in determining the success of a Social Media Marketing campaign.

The adopted strategies can vary significantly depending on the company's objectives and target audience. Some common strategies include creating original and engaging content, regular posting, collaborating with influencers, and using paid advertising to increase brand visibility. Each strategy should be customized based on the specific needs of the company and the characteristics of its target audience.

To evaluate the effectiveness of the adopted strategies, it's important to analyze the results achieved. Key performance indicators to consider include the number of acquired followers, generated engagement (likes, comments, shares), website traffic generated, and lead generation and conversions. The results obtained can be evaluated both quantitatively and qualitatively to understand the actual impact of the Social Media Marketing campaign on the company.

A concrete example of adopted strategies and results achieved in a Social Media Marketing campaign could involve a food and beverage company aiming to increase brand visibility and product sales. To achieve this goal, the company might adopt various strategies, such as creating original and appetizing recipes to share on social media, collaborating with food bloggers and influencers, organizing contests and giveaways to encourage engagement, and using paid advertising to promote their products.

To evaluate the results achieved, the company could monitor the number of followers acquired during the campaign, the engagement generated by published posts, the traffic generated to their website, and most importantly, the actual sales generated through social media. This way, the company can assess the effectiveness of its strategies and make any necessary corrections or improvements to optimize future results.

An essential aspect to consider in evaluating the results achieved is the alignment between the set objectives and the results actually obtained. For example, if the primary goal of the Social Media Marketing campaign was to increase sales, it's crucial to evaluate whether the results obtained actually correspond to that objective. If not, it will be necessary to review the adopted strategies and make adjustments to achieve the set objectives.

Analyzing the adopted strategies and the results achieved is a crucial step in evaluating the effectiveness of a Social Media Marketing campaign and optimizing future results. Through careful and detailed analysis, companies can understand which strategies have been effective and which ones need to be adjusted or enhanced. Only through thorough analysis can businesses derive maximum benefits from Social Media Marketing and ensure the success of their online marketing initiatives.

20. Setting Up Advertising Ads

Social media marketing has become a fundamental tool for companies looking to promote their products and services. Thanks to the widespread popularity of social networks such as Facebook, Instagram, Twitter, and LinkedIn, it's possible to reach a broad audience effectively and targeted.

One of the most important strategies in social media marketing is creating effective advertising campaigns. These campaigns can be set up to achieve various objectives, such as increasing website traffic, generating leads, increasing sales, or raising brand awareness.

Before setting up an advertising campaign on social networks, it's crucial to clearly define the objectives you want to achieve. This step is essential because it will determine the type of ad to create and the audience to target.

Once the objectives are defined, you also need to establish a budget for the campaign. The budget will determine how the campaign will be structured and the costs for clicks, views, and other actions you wish to achieve.

To set up the advertising campaign on social networks, you can use the advertising tools offered directly by social platforms. For example, on Facebook, you can create ads through Facebook Ads Manager, while on Instagram, you can create ads through Instagram Ads. You can set costs for clicks per conversion (CPC) or per 1000 ad views (CPM) depending on the target audience of the app.

Once you've chosen the advertising tools to use, you can define the campaign's target audience. This step is crucial to ensure that ads are shown to the right people. For example, you can target the audience based on age, gender, geographical location, interests, and behaviors.

Moreover, you can use retargeting to show ads to people who have interacted with the brand in the past. Retargeting is an excellent way to regain lost customers and increase conversions.

Once the target audience is defined, you can choose the ad format. Common formats include images, videos, carousels, and slideshows. It's essential to choose a format that suits the ad's content and captures the audience's attention.

In addition to the ad format, it's also important to dcfinc the type of action you want to generate with the advertising campaign. For example, you can set up ads to generate clicks to the website, app installations, lead generation, or engagement.

Once the advertising campaign is set up, it's essential to continuously monitor the ad's performance. You can use the analytical tools offered by social platforms to monitor the number of clicks, views, conversions, and other key metrics.

Based on the collected metrics, you can optimize the advertising campaign to improve ad performance. For example, you can test different ad formats, adjust the target audience, or regulate the budget to maximize campaign performance.

Setting up an advertising campaign on social networks requires careful planning and meticulous optimization. By using advertising tools offered by social platforms and continuously monitoring ad performance, you can achieve effective results and reach your marketing goals.

21. Glossary

Social Media Marketing (SMM) is a discipline that focuses on promoting a brand, product, or service through social media platforms. This marketing approach has become increasingly important in recent years due to the popularity and widespread use of social media among the global population. In this glossary, we will explore key concepts and techniques of Social Media Marketing.

1. Social Media: Social media are online platforms where users can connect, interact, and share content with each other. Some examples of social media include Facebook, Twitter, Instagram, LinkedIn, and TikTok.

2. Social Media Marketing (SMM): Social Media Marketing refers to strategies and activities aimed at promoting a brand, product, or service on social media. These activities may include managing social profiles, paid advertising, engaging with users, and creating

content.

3. Business Profile: A business profile is a social media account created by a company or brand to promote its products or services. Business profiles offer additional functionalities compared to personal accounts, such as performance analytics and the ability to create advertising campaigns.

4. Social Media Advertising: Social media advertising is a form of paid promotion that allows businesses to display advertisements to their target audience on social media platforms. Social media platforms offer various advertising options, including display ads, video ads, and sponsored posts.

5. Engagement: Engagement refers to users' interaction with content published by a brand on social media. High engagement levels may indicate that the content is relevant and interesting to the target audience.

6. Influencer Marketing: Influencer marketing is a form of marketing that involves influential individuals on social media, known as influencers, to promote a brand, product, or service. Influencers have a large follower base and can help increase brand visibility.

7. Hashtag: A hashtag is a word or phrase preceded by the symbol # used to organize and categorize content on social media. Hashtags are often used to increase content visibility and connect it to popular conversations and topics.

8. Engagement Rate: Engagement rate is a measure of the amount of interaction (likes, comments, shares) received on social media content relative to the total number of followers. A high engagement rate may indicate that the content is high quality and engaging for the audience.

9. Analytics: Analytics are data and statistics collected by social media platforms to monitor the performance of social media marketing activities. Analytics provide detailed insights into user engagement, audience demographics, and consumption trends.

10. Call-to-Action (CTA): A call-to-action is an invitation or request made to readers or users to perform a specific action, such as clicking a link, filling out a form, or making a purchase. CTAs are often used to guide users towards conversions.

11. Brand Awareness: Brand awareness refers to the extent to which a brand is recognized and remembered by the target audience. Social Media Marketing can be used to increase brand awareness through content publishing and advertising on social media platforms.

12. Target Audience: The target audience is the group of people targeted by a company's marketing activities. Identifying the target audience is essential for creating targeted and effective content on social media.

13. Content Marketing: Content marketing refers to creating and distributing relevant, high-quality content to attract and engage the target audience. Social Media Marketing is an effective channel for distributing content through social media platforms.

14. Brand Voice: Brand voice is the style of communication and personality of the brand expressed through content published on social media. Defining a consistent brand voice is important for creating a strong and recognizable brand image.

15. Social Listening: Social listening is the monitoring of brand conversations and mentions on social media to understand people's attitudes and opinions towards the

brand. Social listening can help identify improvement opportunities and respond promptly to customer comments.

16. Return on Investment (ROI): Return on Investment is a measure of the profitability of a social media marketing campaign relative to the costs incurred. Calculating ROI is important for evaluating the effectiveness of Social Media Marketing activities and optimizing future strategies.

17. Brand Advocacy: Brand advocacy refers to the active promotion and support of a brand by loyal and satisfied customers. Social Media Marketing can encourage brand advocacy through sharing positive experiences and user-generated content.

18. Competitor Analysis: Competitor analysis is the process of evaluating the strategies and performance of direct competitors on social media platforms. Monitoring competitors can help identify differentiation opportunities and

remain competitive in the market.

19. Social Media Management: Social media management is the activity of managing and monitoring business profiles on social media. Social media management platforms allow scheduling posts, monitoring engagement, and efficiently responding to user comments.

20. Social Media Strategy: Social media strategy is a detailed plan that defines objectives, target audience, tactics, and measurement metrics for social media marketing activities. A well-defined strategy is essential for achieving effective and measurable results on social media platforms.

Social Media Marketing is a continuously changing and evolving field, and adopting new trends and technologies is crucial to remain competitive in the digital landscape. Understanding and applying key concepts of Social Media Marketing can help businesses achieve their marketing goals and establish a strong and influential online presence.

Index

1. Introduction pg.4

2. Benefits of Social Media Marketing for Businesses pg.8

3. Main Tools and Platforms of Social Media Marketing Analysis of Key Social Platforms (Facebook, Instagram, X (formerly Twitter), LinkedIn, Pinterest, YouTube) pg.13

4. Social Media Management and Monitoring Tools Visual and Video Content Creation Tools pg.18

5. Defining Social Media Marketing Objectives pg.24

6. Defining Content and Engagement Strategies pg.28

7. Planning Social Media Advertising Campaigns pg.32

8. Creating and Managing Company Profiles on Social Media pg.37

9. Monitoring Activities and Performance Indicators pg.41

10. Responding to User Interactions and Crisis Management pg.45

11. Creating Effective Content for Social Media pg.50

12. Most Effective Content Types on Each Social Media Platform pg.53

13. Best Practices for Creating Visual and Video Content pg.57

14. Tools for Creating and Scheduling Content pg.62

15. Performance Analysis and Reporting pg.66

16. Monitoring campaign and brand performance on social media pg.71

17. Creation of periodic reports and analysis of results pg.75

18. Strategies pg.79

19. Analysis of Adopted Strategies and Achieved Results pg.93

20. Setting Up Advertising Ads pg.97

21. Glossary pg.101

www.ingramcontent.com/pod-product-compliance
Lightning Source LLC
Chambersburg PA
CBHW071937210526
45479CB00002B/718